To Andrew
from Uncle William

With special thanks to Laura
for making this book possible

東苑海鮮菜

TO CHINATOWN

到華埠

CHINESE AMERICAN

號 中 西 雜

William Low

CHINATOWN

Developmental Studies Center

For all permission inquiries contact Henry Holt
Books for Young Readers, 175 Fifth Avenue,
New York, NY 10010.

This Developmental Studies Center edition is
published by arrangement with Henry Holt
Books for Young Readers.

Developmental Studies Center
1250 53rd Street, Suite 3
Emeryville, CA 94608-2965
800.666.7270 * fax: 510.464.3670
devstu.org

First Edition—1997 / Typography by Martha Rago
The artist used oil paints on board to create
illustrations for this book.

ISBN 978-1-61003-224-7
Printed in China

1 2 3 4 5 6 7 8 9 10 RRD 20 19 18 17 16 15 14

I live in Chinatown with my mother, father, and grandmother. Our apartment is above the Chinese American grocery store.

Every morning Grandma and I go
for a walk through Chinatown. We hold
hands before we cross the street. "Watch out
for cars, Grandma," I tell her.

6

Most days the tai chi class has already begun by the time we get to the park. Students, young and old, move in the sunlight like graceful dancers.

We always stop and say hello to Mr. Wong, the street cobbler. If our shoes need fixing, Mr. Wong can do the job.
  "Just like new, and at a good price, too," says Mr. Wong.

Chinatown really wakes up when
the delivery trucks arrive. Men with
handcarts move quickly over
the sidewalks and into the stores.

13

Every day Grandma and I walk past the Dai-Dai Restaurant. Roasted chicken is my favorite, but Grandma likes duck best.

When it gets cold outside and Grandma needs to make medicinal soup, we visit the herbal shop. Inside it is dark and smells musty. The owner, Mr. Chung, is bagging dried roots and herbs.

"Winter is here," says Grandma. "We must get our strength up."

Sometimes Grandma and I go for lunch at a seafood restaurant. I like to watch the fish swim in the tank. Grandma says, "You won't find fresher fish than those in Chinatown."

The kitchen in the restaurant is a noisy place. Hot oil sizzles, vegetables crackle, and woks clang and bang. The cooks shout to be heard.

At the outdoor market I can barely move. But we go there because Grandma likes to buy fresh snapping crabs for dinner. When the crabs seem furious, Grandma is pleased. "The angrier the crabs, the tastier the meat," she says.

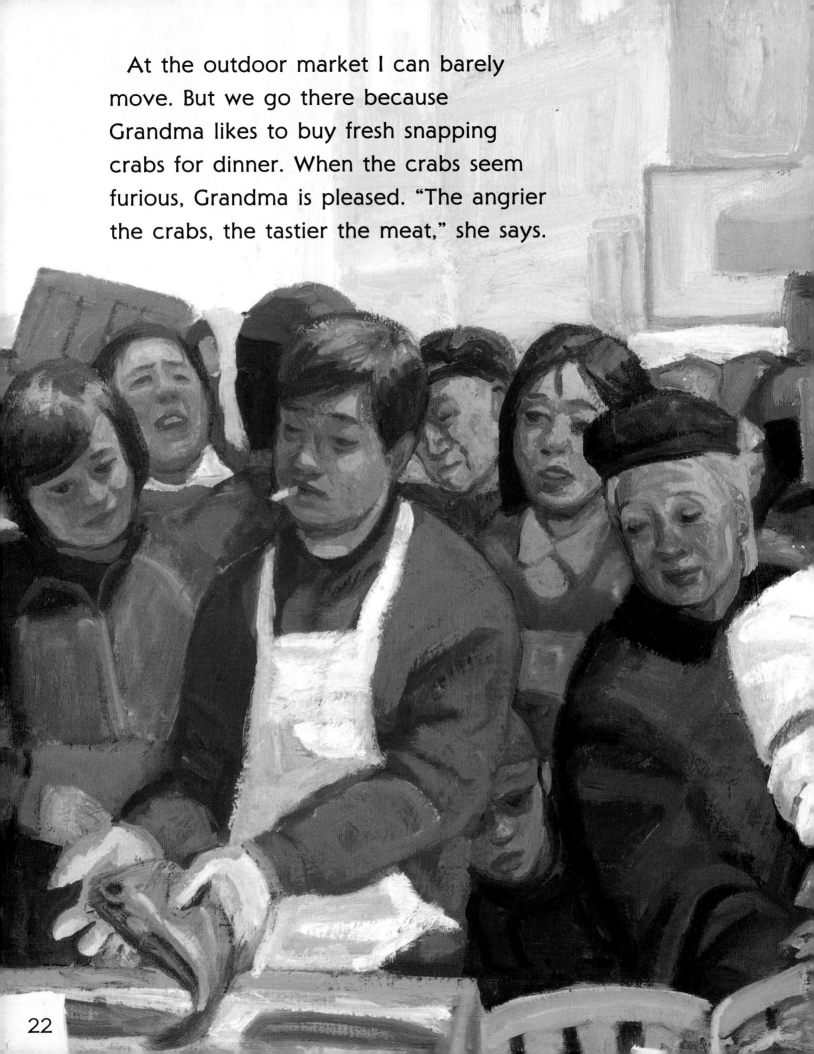

23

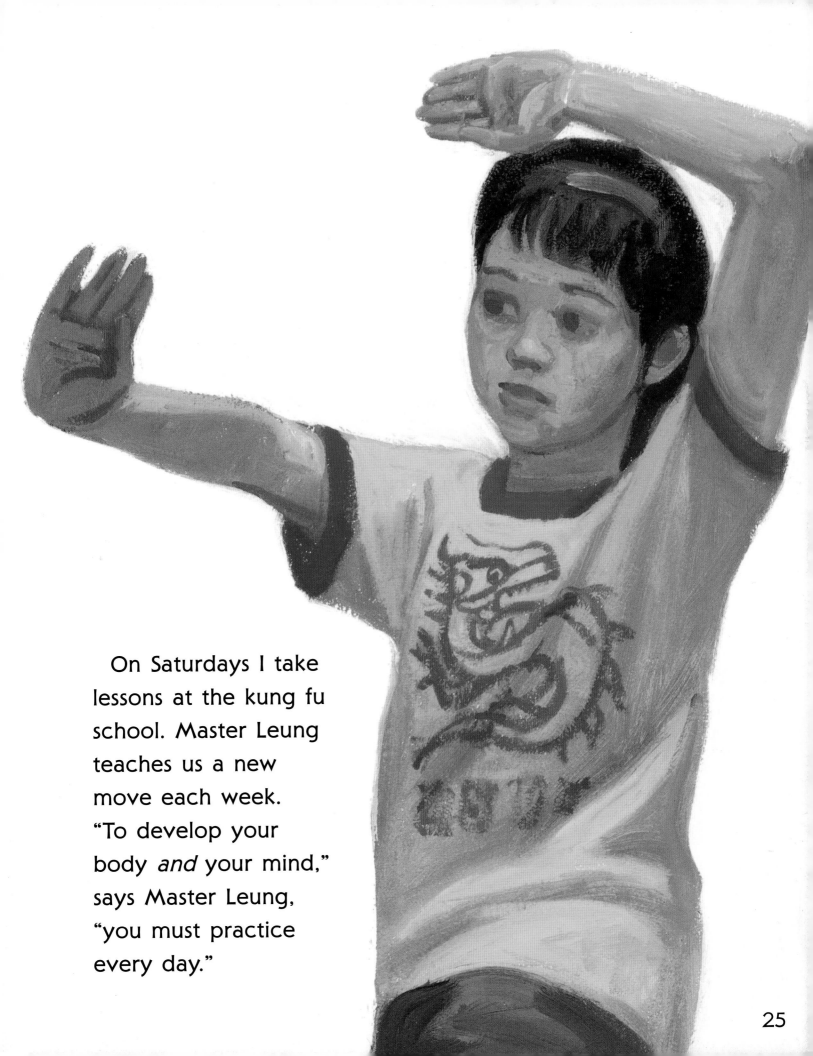

On Saturdays I take lessons at the kung fu school. Master Leung teaches us a new move each week. "To develop your body *and* your mind," says Master Leung, "you must practice every day."

My favorite holiday is Chinese New Year.
During the celebrations the streets of
Chinatown are always crowded. "Be sure
to stay close by," Grandma says.

On New Year's Day the older kids from my kung fu school march to the beat of thumping drums. Grandma and I try to find a good place to watch, and I tell her that next year I'll be marching, too.

The New Year's Day parade winds noisily through the streets. "Look, Grandma!" I say. "Here comes the lion."

Firecrackers explode when the lion dance is over. I turn to Grandma, take her hand, and say, "*Gung hay fat choy*, Grandma."

She smiles at me. "And a happy new year to you, too."